Born Into Trauma

Tia Martin

Copyright © 2025 by **Tia Martin**

All rights reserved. This book is protected by the copyright laws of United States of America. No part of this book may be reproduced, distributed, or transmitted in any form or by any means, including photocopying, recording, or other electronic or mechanical methods, without the prior written permission of the publisher. Permission will be granted upon request.

ISBN: 978-1-6653-1076-5

This ISBN is the property of BookLogix for the express purpose of sales and distribution of this title. BookLogix is not responsible for the writing, editing, or design/appearance of this book. The content of this book is the property of the copyright holder only. BookLogix does not hold any ownership of the content of this book and is not liable in any way for the materials contained within. The views and opinions expressed in this book are the property of the Author/Copyright holder, and do not necessarily reflect those of BookLogix.

Library of Congress Control Number: 2025908599

Table of Contents

Introduction 1

Chapter 1

Unchartered Territory 11

Chapter 2

Broken Home 20

Chapter 3

Silent Nights 27

Chapter 4

Distraught 31

Chapter 5

The Unexpected 39

Chapter 6

Sweet Memories 48

Chapter 7

The Separation 54

Chapter 8

Moving On 70

Chapter 9

Motivation 76

Chapter 10
The Straw That Broke the Camel's Back 90

A Letter to My First Assailant 108
A Letter to My Ex-Husband 111
A Letter to God 114
A Letter to My Husband 118

Introduction

I was born on September 16, 1983, in Cordele, GA. My parents, Walter and Cora Roberts, got married right before I was born—meaning my mom was pregnant with me. I have three other siblings: an older brother, Rob, and two younger sisters, Suela and Keo. My older brother has a different father. So, I am the oldest of my father's three girls and the second oldest of my mother's four children. I myself have six wonderful children, five of which I birthed. My oldest is 20 years old, and the youngest is 10 months. I got pregnant with my first child at the age of 22 and had her when I turned 23. She was born in 2006. At the time, I was a girlfriend figuring out my way through life while working and going to school. I got my associate's degree from Middle GA college in 2005. I was finally able to move out of the town I was raised in, Hawkinsville, to Warner Robins in 2007. In Warner Robins, I had my second daughter the same year. I ended up getting married to their father after being together for four years in 2009. The following year, I had my first son in 2010. While pregnant with him, I attended Argosy University and obtained my bachelor's degree in Business Administration in 2011. From here, I attended Strayer University and got my Master of Science in Accounting.

Growing up was a bit hard. We moved around a lot, plus my parents did a lot of arguing and physical fighting. We stayed in a house for a year or less, and then we were out of there. I didn't have too much time to have any childhood friends before becoming a teenager due to the moves. I got teased because not only was I a crybaby but a nerd as well. I was a straight-A student. I desired to learn and pass everything. We had an okay life. We weren't rich, but we weren't that poor either. We didn't really experience poor living until the year 1995 when I was 12 years old, the same time my mother decided to leave my father finally. She did it so smoothly. It was during the summertime, and my mother instructed us to pack because we were going to stay with our grandmother for the rest of the summer. Little did we know that was the last time that we would reside in Pineview, GA.

We mostly lived in a two- to three-bedroom home. Once, after my parents' separation, we lived in a one-bedroom duplex. My mother is a hard-working woman. She worked, took care of the house, and made sure we (her children) had all of our essential needs. My father worked and partied a lot; he was a part of that song I used to hear called *Papa Was a Rollin' Stone*, except he did come home every night. I recall he would come home at all times of the night and start fights with my mom. They both drank and, unbeknownst to me at the time, participated in drugs. I rarely saw her drunk but saw him drunk almost daily. She got beat up a lot by him. A lot of times, I felt like he was just upset and wanted a punching bag to take his frustrations out on because, as a kid, I didn't see my mom do anything hurtful to him. As a pre-teen, I felt like he would come home to beat on her because one of his flings probably pissed him off. I don't know the real answers to why they argued so much. I never thought about asking nor too much cared for the real answer. I would hear their arguments when we were supposed to be asleep. I was a momma's girl, so I clung to my mother. I was always somewhere nearby. I hated to hear her cry. Every time they argued, I was all ears to make sure she was okay. I was too afraid of my father to tell him to back off, so all I did was listen and silently cry with her.

My brother has a different father. My father helped to raise him since he was one year old. My father was my big brother's only father figure in his life, but it didn't seem to me like the father-son relationship was a good one. I say that because my father had some pretty mean technics for raising his children. He told my brother that he was responsible for us girls. He also told me the same thing: that we were all responsible for each other and that if one got in trouble, we all got in trouble. But I know my brother got the worst of it because he is the oldest. Keo and I used to follow our brother around everywhere he went. He hated it, but if we veered off and did our own thing without anyone knowing, we would get a good beating. Back in the 90s, we had clotheslines to hang out our clothes to dry. One day, I heard my father yelling at my brother outside by the clothesline. I saw him punch my brother in the chest. Rob started crying and grabbed his chest. My father yelled and told him to be still and take it like a man, and then he hit him again. I swung the door open and told him to quit hitting on my brother. We were living in a trailer at the time. My father turned to me and said, "Shut up unless you want to take the licks for him." I closed the door, peeked through the little circle window of the door, and started crying. I was terrified of my father. He was mean to all of us. I remember we were all sitting in the living room and felt the whole trailer shake. I thought it was an earthquake. My mother jumped up and ran to the back door. We followed. She screamed his name and persisted in trying to help him. The big shake was because he was drunk and, I guess, fell asleep while pulling into the yard, thereby crashing into the trailer. That was scary. There are so many more memories of the drunkenness that was traumatizing. The most unforgettable moment was the whole family coming back home from a friend's house in a different town. My parents were drinking and having themselves a good ole time. We all piled up in the car and headed home. My father was driving. The next thing I remember, my mother and he got into a heated argument. My father got so furious. My mother screamed, grabbed the wheel, and asked him what the hell he was thinking. That was a very scary moment. Imagine you and two of your siblings sitting in the back seat as young children, and no one has even reached the pre-teen stage; your parents are in the front seat, and your father tries to drive the car over a big, tall cliff, but your mother comes through and saves everyone. I was definitely not ready to die that day, and I am so thankful that my mother was able to react fast. That was the first of many close-to-losing-my-life events.

My baby sister missed a lot of the crazy two-parent home shenanigans. She unfortunately grew up with one parent for the majority of her life. I got the best of both worlds and can honestly say that even though we were extremely poor, I was more comfortable with my parents separated. The abuse, alcohol, drugs, beatings, and close calls were all too much to bear. My big brother was eventually allowed to venture off on his own and leave us behind. So, I continued practicing being the protector of my two younger siblings. Keo was a year behind me, so there wasn't much for me to raise with her. She actually told me one time that she wished she was the big sister. I mean, it kind of made sense since she acted like it. I was too fragile and shy to even think about taking on the role of a big sister. All I had was the title. Keo demanded attention wherever she went. She was not only mean but fought a lot in school. Nobody dared to mess with her twice or they knew what was coming. She was what the older folks called "Hell on Wheels" because she didn't take no mess from nobody. I envied that about her because I dreamed of not being a pushover. I only wished I had the courage she did. I, on the other hand, got bullied a lot. So other people in my family fought my battles for me, including Keo.

When my mother had Suela, that was my chance to be a caretaker, provider, and protector. She came out looking just like me. Even with our big gap in age difference, people still thought we looked just like twins, so we kind of started telling people we were twins. Keo and I used to dress up like twins all the time. When Suela came along, we all dressed up like triplets. It was so much fun. I practically raised my baby sister. When my mother came home from the hospital, she didn't have to do anything but heal. Taking care of Suela was a must for me. I needed to take care of her for my mother's sake and my own sake. She exercised and fed us while I took care of Suela the best way I could. She was a spoiled little brat too. Daddy didn't whoop her like he whooped the older three children. She got laughed at with all the bad stuff she did. I was so angry with them for that. I mean, we weren't allowed to sneeze wrong or all of us were going to get it. So I figured I had to discipline her myself. I never went to the extreme my father did, but I made sure she was punished for her wrongdoings in a healthier, loving way. That girl was so spoiled that it was ridiculous. She was a tough one, even with the discipline.

She got into everything and got away with everything with the adults.

I did my best with Suela. I was probably a little too quiet for her though because she was very outgoing. I also stayed sick a lot due to my health issues and stayed in the house due to afraid of facing the world. My siblings would always try to get me to come outside, and I would always say no. It was my mother who would have to force me out of the house. I admit I had fun once I went, but the fact remained the same: I was scared to interact with people outside of my own home. When I did go out, I would go wherever Keo wanted us to go, or we would follow our brother and try to hang with his friends. I would probably throw out a few suggestions here and there, but I mainly followed Rob. We didn't really go over to too many friends' houses; our main chill spots were at a family member's house. We grew up with our fraternal family. I didn't really grow up with my mom's family until I turned 12. If I wasn't forced out of the house, I would sit with my mom and watch TV or watch her cook and cry. I would ask what was wrong, and her response would be, "Nothing, baby." So, sitting in silence was our thing. She didn't really like crying in front of us. I would always find her in the kitchen cooking and crying or washing dishes and crying. I don't think my other siblings noticed our mom's constant crying because they were always too eager to go outside to play, while I preferred to stay close to my mother. I knew my mom was having a hard time most days. So when she got pregnant with Suela, I immediately took on the role of being the big sister so she could focus on healing.

Chapter 1

Unchartered Territory

As a child, I was too timid to talk. I was afraid to get in trouble in any way possible. I did everything I possibly could to not get in trouble. I still got in trouble though. My upbringing was if any of my other siblings got in trouble, I was going to get into trouble as well because we were all responsible for one another. I would sit in the house, and the next thing I knew, my father would call me and tell me it was my turn for my beating. I was shocked; why did I still have to get a beating when I was not even there? His response was, "Well, you should have been there to stop them." He would whip us each for what felt like hours at a time. My mom would have to intervene each time and let him know that was enough. He was like the energizer bunny; he kept going and going and going. It was a nightmare.

I also did not do much talking because I was afraid someone would see my flaws; they would know my secrets, and they would be so mad at me for what I had experienced. At the time, I had no idea, but I had experienced trauma before I was even born. My mom and dad got into one of their many fights, and he kicked her right in the stomach while she was pregnant with me. I was head down, so in the midst of him kicking her, he kicked me right dead smack in the head. It seems like all odds were against me before birth. On top of that, my mom confirmed that I was a crack baby. So here I am, born with a hole in my heart, diagnosed with a heart murmur, a soft spot on top of my head that was a little abnormal due to a blow to the head before birth, and probably born with drugs in my system. I'm not sure if they tested my mother for drugs back in those days, but to my knowledge, my parents did every drug there was to do in the 80s. So, not only were they alcoholics but drug addicts also. I was aware that my parents drank alcohol, but I was very naïve about my mother doing any type of drug. I mean, she worked hard, managed the house, and made sure we kept up with our schoolwork and whatever else adult things that had to be done.

I was what some called weird and a nerd. All I wanted to do was get good grades, stay out of trouble, and stay up under my mother. I couldn't control the things that were happening around me in my life, so I controlled what I ate, which can be very hard growing up in a household that heavily believes in "Eat what I cook or don't eat anything at all." And they better not see none of that unwanted food in the trash either. I was slick though. I would be the last person to get up from the table and put my unwanted food under items already in the trashcan. So many nights, I went hungry but never starved. I also would tap the doorknob three times with long sleeves on before I entered a room and counted my footsteps from the time I woke up to the time I went to bed. I was so good that I would stop walking and counting to converse and then continue counting where I left off. I actually had fun counting. It was relieving and somewhat meditative.

We didn't really grow up with my family on my mom's side, but we did go to visit my grandmother from time to time. We used to have so much fun visiting my grandmother in the country. We encountered so many scary moments and loved hearing the tales of the different encounters my mom and aunts experienced, like seeing an actual man on the moon, having their backs ridden by witches, and bears knocking at the door at the same time every night. Now, I personally heard a knock at the door one night, and my grandmother calmly said, "Girl, you better not answer that door. It's a bear that comes and knocks on the door around the same time every night." So I didn't, and whatever it was went away.

My grandmother lived right in the front of a field. That field had cotton, field peas, butter beans, okra, or whatever the harvest was at the time of year. We had fun going over and helping our mom and grandmother work out in the fields. We would run up and down the rows and hide between the vegetables. We couldn't play too much because the adults were working, and if we were going to be out there, we had to do a little work in between playing. Weekly, we would watch the airplanes fly over the fields and spray chemicals. We even felt like we were getting chased by the planes from time to time because we would be out in the fields playing and the planes would fly low to the ground and chase us with their sprayer. We had some really fun times.

I remember we would go visit my aunt, my mother's sister, whenever we came to town. Sadly, she died from a fatal car accident. When we got the news, we were very young and didn't really understand what was happening. My brother did though. Keo and I saw him cry and go lay on the bed at our grandmother's house, so we followed him and did the same thing because we thought that was what we were supposed to do. I mean, we loved and missed her too. We just didn't understand that we would never see her again. My brother understood, so we just did what he did and cried together. The visits to my aunt's house were pleasant. At one point and time, those visits became a nightmare.

Back in those days, children were not allowed to sit around adults nor even speak if they were not being spoken too. My mom would send us to the back room to play with our cousins. I don't think Suela was born at the time, so it was Rob, Keo and myself. We would go and listen to music in our big cousin's room. He would play all the cool music. We looked up to our big cousin. One day, our big cousin turned the music up really loud and sent Rob and Keo out of the room. He told me to stay so he could show me something. I was between the ages of four and five then. I hate that I stayed because this became a routine when we visited. I don't recall how many times he would send them out of the room. I just know I hated to see them go. Then, one awful day, I was in so much pain, and all I could see was a big smirk on his face. When he finished, I ran out of the room and told my mother and aunt that "he" pulled my pants down. I didn't know what else to say. My mom and aunt turned around and yelled, "Boy, don't be pulling this girl pants down." Needless to say, that was the last time I was physically raped and the beginning of a lifelong mental and emotional torture. I felt horrible because I did not feel like the situation was handled well enough. I was young. I didn't know what was going on, but I did know that something was not right. From that moment, I felt invisible. I felt like I was not even worth the bother anymore to anyone, so being in the shadows and staying out of everyone's way was the best way that I was going to have to protect myself.

This was when I became a cry baby and distant from the world. I was even peeing in the bed. I became so mad at my mother for not protecting me. I had no idea what she was supposed to have done, but I knew saying a few words without looking into what was happening was not it. I also felt somewhat safe at her side because no one would dare touch me while she was looking. It was weird to me, but that was my way of dealing with whatever was going on with me—stay by my mother's side, and that would minimize or stop anything else from happening.

I was in kindergarten, and a classmate asked me why I had breasts. She thought it was so funny. I, on the other hand, felt embarrassed and like an outsider. I honestly had not realized that my body was different from all the other children's. I started paying attention and noticed that I was the only girl in that school with breasts. It was the beginning of my low self-esteem and shame toward my very own body. From that moment forward, I began labeling myself as the ugly girl. The ugly girl was all that I saw when I looked in the mirror.

As an adult, I realized that learning starts in the home and that family can build you up or tear you down within the blink of an eye. You may have a favorite uncle or cousin that you look up to, not knowing that the whole time, they are looking at you like a piece of meat, waiting to pick the right time, the right moment to strike and take your innocence along with everything else that follows. I didn't feel like this fit the description for every single person, but my mind was telling me to trust nobody, absolutely no one. And picking up the pieces was not the abuser's problem; their main focus is satisfying whatever desire it is that they are trying to reach at that moment while causing lifelong damage.

I was young. I had no idea what was going on or how it would impact my life. I did my part; I told my mother and his mother. However, I was not satisfied with the full results. I felt like it wasn't enough, but at least it stopped. I mean, what was a four- to five-year-old scared little girl going to do? I didn't know how to tell my mother to ask me those prying questions to figure out if her baby girl had been hurt in any way, shape, form, or fashion. I didn't know how to tell my mother to check my private parts or take me to the doctor to see if I had been sexually assaulted. I didn't know how to tell my mother to stop making us go to the back room to play. I just didn't know. As I got older, I started telling myself that maybe my mother didn't know either.

Chapter 2

Broken Home

I was raised in a two-parent household up until the age of 11. I turned 12 later that year. My father was hard on us, especially my big brother since he was the oldest and a boy. He got it double time. I didn't approve of our upbringing at all, but who was I to tell my parents we were too young to see and experience the things that were happening? My father liked to drink. I remember he would come home drunk just about every night. Some nights, I would hear them arguing. It would even get as bad as seeing them fighting. My father always won, and my mother always ended up crying, sometimes even bleeding. There were so many arguments and fighting. It was hard to even try to keep count because it was probably daily what seemed to me for the entire 11-12 years they were together.

We got whoopings daily from my father, more like beatings. My mother would whoop us occasionally, but my father felt like it was necessary every single day. The sad part about all of this was that I was a good child. I was too scared and timid to get into any trouble. But for some odd reason unknown to me at the time, I still deserved a whooping. My father felt it was necessary because he was trying to teach us that we should be there for each other. So, if one child got caught doing something they had no business doing, then we all had to get in trouble because we should have been there to stop the other sibling from doing wrong. I stayed in the house a lot. So I imagine I got my whoopings because I should have been outside to tell my older brother and younger sister that they shouldn't be doing whatever it was that they were doing. I recall I was outside one time playing hide and go seek—the kid game, not the mannish one. We all got a whooping because my younger sister and I were hiding from our brother on the other side of the bushes.

So, let me give you a small visual. We lived in a single-wide, two-bedroom trailer in Fitzgerald, GA. My younger sister and I had a room. My parents had a room. My brother kept his things in our closet but slept in the living room. Ain't no telling what he was seeing after dark. I was hearing a lot of things, but he was older and I am sure he saw plenty. Next door to the right of our trailer was another single-wide trailer. Then, there was this fence made out of bushes that separated my neighbor's single-wide trailer from this big, beautiful brick home on the other side. We never bothered that neighbor. I do not even know who lived there or anything. I do not remember anyone coming or going from that residence. But I do know my siblings and I got our butts torn up because my sister and I hid in the neighbor's yard on the other side, what appeared to be the forbidden bushes. I still don't fully understand to this day why we had to get a whooping. We were children playing an innocent game, having a good ole' time, and not bothering anyone. Who knew a friendly, innocent game of hide and seek would land all three of us one of my father's daily whoopings? Often, my mother would have to stop him because he would whoop us nonstop. My mother saved us plenty of days. For some reason, when my father whooped us, he didn't know how to stop. I was glad my mother was there to stop him. Those whoopings with his thick leather cow belt hurt us badly. So, I had no intention of getting into any trouble at all. But it didn't matter. If one person got into trouble, no matter how big or small, we all got into trouble.

We grew up poor, but we didn't know we were poor. My mother maintained our household flawlessly. She made sure we had a good Christmas every year. I remember one year, for Christmas, this nice lady brought a big black trash bag full of toys to our house. It was at that moment I realized we were not rich and Momma needed assistance to help keep us happy. She cried that day. She was so happy that her children were going to have a good Christmas, and it was my best Christmas ever as a child. Momma also made sure our birthdays were celebrated every single year. We would share parties, but our birthdays were acknowledged separately. We didn't have name-brand clothes and shoes, but we were dressed decent, presentable, and clean daily.

We moved around a lot. Both my parents worked, but we still had to move around as children. I didn't understand it. I needed stability. I didn't like change. So, I stopped trying to make friends. I mean, what was the point? We were just going to move again anyway. We only stayed in a home for a year, and then we were out of there. That made it hard to find friends and keep them because we didn't rely on social media heavily back in those days. We had home phones and pay phones. My friends were my family. It didn't matter where we moved; my family would be somewhere near, or we would go visit them. I know it seems strange for some people, but I have always been closer to the family on my father's side. We grew up around them more than the family on my mom's side. I didn't really meet any of my family on my mother's side until I was around 12. I mean, I knew my aunts and their children, but that was all. I kept that bond going with my paternal family because we were around them the most. I'm big on family, and it was so important to me to keep the relationships going on both sides, new and old relationships. My father was a family man. Back then, being a family man, to me, was living in the same household as your wife and children. I heard him tell his friends also that he was a family man. Now, don't get me wrong, he loved his children and wife. From my young point of view, he also loved to work, drink, and party. I would find my mother in the kitchen cooking and crying. I wanted to help her so many times, but I knew that would end up with us getting a bad whooping for interfering in grown folks' business. Lord knows I hated getting into trouble, and I was afraid of my father. I wouldn't dare to raise a hand up to him. None of us did—except my baby sister. She was a brave little girl. Our parents didn't raise a hand up to her, so she had no experience with the fear that my father instilled in us. She was fearless and didn't go for Daddy putting his hands on our mother. She would jump on his back, bite him, kick him, punch him, whatever she felt was necessary to get him off of Mom. She almost got knocked out one time. She jumped on his back, and he threw her off of him, not realizing it was her until she flew across the room. That calmed him down a little bit, but it didn't fully stop him from whatever his purpose was at that moment. I admired her for those moments because she was the bravest of us all.

Chapter 3

Silent Nights

Sleep was never a friend of mine. I can't recall if I've had bad dreams nightly or just regularly. I just know that it was hard and scary to fall asleep. When I finally fell sleep, it was hard to wake up. I am still not a morning person to this day. I sleep a little better now but still find it hard to get up. I was roughly in the third grade when I was still wetting the bed. Sometimes, I would have these weird dreams of toilets and wet the bed. Other nights, it would be nightmares that caused me to wet the bed. I recall waking up in the middle of the night to sneak to the bathroom and change my underwear. I don't think I ever changed my sheets; I only recall changing my underwear. What mattered to me then was that once my parents woke me up for school, I would be dry and not wet to avoid getting a good beating. I did this religiously for many nights. I became a pro at wetting the bed, getting up in the middle of the night before everyone else woke up, cleaning up, and getting back in bed as if nothing ever happened. I was so good. I don't even think my parents had a clue about what was going on.

I remember one night I went to the bathroom in the middle of the night after I dreamt I was on the toilet. The warmth is what woke me up. It was already close to the time to go to school. So I got out of bed, embarrassed and ashamed but still knowing that no one would ever find out. I slithered to the bathroom, washed up, and got dressed for school. I didn't need to use the toilet at home because I had soiled the sheets. I went on to school as if nothing had ever happened. It was just a normal day for me. I was quiet, shy, and not looking anyone in the eyes. I did have a best friend at the time. I was a straight-A student—a nerd, if you will. Nothing was special nor out of the ordinary to me. I thought it was a normal day—laughing with my friend and ignoring everyone else. Again, I didn't have to use the bathroom at home because I had done so in bed. Then, it was time to take a bathroom break at school. I went to the bathroom and used one of the tiny stalls they had for the elementary students. It was at that moment I realized I had been at school all day without underwear. There were other girls in the bathroom as well. I refused to come out until they left. I felt so exposed. The unique part about this whole situation is that no one knew I was at school without underwear. My insecurities were getting the best of me. All these emotions were brewing so rapidly and fast. All the while, no one knew that I had forgotten to put on new and clean underwear. No one knew that I was being raped by my first cousin every time we came to visit them. No one knew that I was getting whoopings nearly every single day. No one knew that my parents were physically and verbally fighting all the time. No one knew!

As I write this, my breathing is becoming a little harder. The air feels hot and slim coming into my body. My chest is becoming tighter, and a little pain is trying to set in. That was a huge moment for me that happens often. The entire situation with me forgetting to put on underwear was how the rest of my life was lived up to the age of 30. Every little or big event led me to believe I was being exposed, believing that everyone in the world, including the ones I loved dearly, would hate me because of what had happened to me.

I take a moment to check in and breathe while reassuring myself that I am safe…

Inhale…hold…1, 2, 3, 4, 5, 6, 7, 8, 9, 10…Exhale… I repeat this as many times as I need to until I feel my body relax.

Chapter 4

Distraught

As I mentioned before, I grew up in a dysfunctional two-parent household until the age of eleven. My parents fought metaphorically like cats and dogs. I know they loved us, but they just had strange ways of showing love to each other. As a child, I was glued to my mother's hip, too scared to roam anywhere else. She would sometimes make me go outside to play, but other times, she let me sit by her while I read my books as she cooked or watched television. My siblings always begged me to come outside and play, but I didn't care about facing the outside world—it was never good to me. I got bullied a lot and cried often. My brother loved calling me a crybaby, and truthfully, he was right. I cried over everything. Sometimes, I wonder if my brother knew he was being sent out of the room so that I could be raped by our big cousin, whom we looked up to. Then again, my brother was only a year older than me. Logically, if I didn't know what was going on, he probably didn't either. We didn't know the signs. No one talked to us about good touch, bad touch, child abuse, molestation, or even rape. No one told us that family could be not only loving but cruel too. We weren't warned, prepared, or taught anything about these things. We just had to figure them out as we faced life.

So, yes, I cried a lot. The pain was so unreal and unbearable that tears appeared in every situation except the one they needed to be expressed in. Those feelings were buried, with attempts to forget. It hurt being called a crybaby all the time, especially when my big brother said it, because I wanted so badly to tell him why I cried so much. But we were children, and I didn't know how to tell him, and I didn't want him to be mad at me for what our cousin did to me.

We walked almost everywhere with our mother. She did her best to take good care of us. She made sure we had decent clothes, a hot meal, a place to sleep, and a good education. We were not allowed to bring home Cs or Ds. I remember bringing home a B once and crying so hard because I thought I would get a whipping for not getting an A. My mom wasn't even upset, but my brother laughed at me. To him, crying over just a B was unnecessary; to me, it was a big deal, and I had to cry. I felt like such a failure. I was ugly, worthless, and just wasting space on this earth. All I had were my good grades. I needed that A; bringing home a B wasn't good enough. I was the smartest kid in my class, even the teacher's pet. I was an awesome reader and sometimes speed-read, which got me in trouble. I read so fast that the teacher threatened to fail me because she couldn't keep up. It both tickled and upset me because my A was at stake. I wasn't going to risk a bad grade, so I complied and slowed down my reading so she and the other students could hear and understand the words. Besides being a good reader, I was also a great speller and won the spelling bee. I felt so proud of myself. I knew I could do it, but the recognition felt amazing—a high I longed for but rarely felt.

Back to my mom. We walked everywhere with her. No matter where she went, she took us with her. We would go to the DFACS office with her. That was one big building with no elevator. We had to walk up what felt like 20 flights of stairs. I think that was my first experience with a fear of heights. I looked down when we reached the floor we were going to and felt dizzy and queasy in the stomach. Heights have never been the same since. One day, Momma walked my two siblings and me to visit Daddy at his job. He drove forklifts. He let all three of us drive the forklift. The baby girl wasn't born yet. I was so excited. Going to Daddy's workplace was always fun. I think it was a lumberjack company. Piles of wood planks were all over the place. So many places to hide and climb. That day, Daddy decided to let us all take turns and drive the forklift. I was overly excited and ready to cut some corners in that big old thing. My brother and younger sister did so well. I couldn't wait until it was my turn to show off my skills. My turn finally came. I sat on my daddy's lap. He turned on the forklift, put his foot on the brakes, and asked me if I was ready. I was *sooo* excited. I put my little hands on that steering wheel and said, "Yes, Daddy." I took the wheel. He pressed the gas, and boom, I ran straight into the pile of wood planks that was right in front of me. Oh boy. My daddy was furious and vowed that I would never drive it again. He stayed true to his word. My siblings did what siblings do; they laughed at me, and of course, I cried.

One day, my mother came home from work crying and scared. I was so worried. I could not bear to see my mother in so much pain. I overheard her tell my daddy that his friend tried to rape her. He offered her a ride home from work. She accepted the ride, then had to jump out of the car (I assume while it was still moving because she was a little scarred up and dirty) and run straight home. My daddy was so mad. He jumped in the car with all of us, and we drove around looking for this so-called friend. We finally found him, and my daddy got out of the car and confronted him with a knife cut to the chest. My mother was right behind him, yelling and screaming. Meanwhile, we (the children) sat in the car, watched, and soaked up all the chaos. Suddenly, I saw my mom and dad run to the trunk and get a BB gun that was back there. While they were in the trunk, the guy swung a bat and hit both my parents in the head. The next thing I knew, blood was streaming from both my parents' faces. I guess neither one got the chance to shoot the gun because their heads were split open. I can't recall what happened after that; my brain was stuck on seeing blood run down both my parents' faces. After all the excitement and chaos, Momma drove us home. She dropped Daddy and us off and went to the hospital to get her head stitched up. Daddy didn't want to go to the hospital. He sat home in the dark with a shirt pressed on his head. My siblings and I hid behind a broken-down car in our backyard and cried together. We stayed there until Momma got back. That experience was frightening and traumatizing.

There were plenty more frightening and traumatizing situations. There was a time when Daddy came home with his mouth wired shut. Momma had to blend up all of his food so he could suck it up through a straw. I couldn't stop staring at how different he looked. He left home for work, I think, perfectly fine and came home hours later with a broken jaw. The story is that he got jumped by a bunch of racist men. That was very believable in the times that we grew up because that is all I heard them talk about. That beating left his face swollen, and he was unable to talk. He drooled so badly. His communication with us was on a notepad. We would talk to him, and he would respond by writing down what he had to say. I wonder if he ever got those men that jumped on him or if it was one of those situations where he just had to take a loss.

I wondered about a lot of things growing up and still to this day. Talking was definitely not my strong suit. Even writing was a challenge because I used as few words as possible. It didn't matter if I was in a verbal conversation or had to write a school report. I always got straight to the point. Following up and asking questions about someone's personal life was just not my thing.

That could easily end up in a very uncomfortable conversation. So, I just wondered.

Chapter 5

The Unexpected

We moved to Pineview, GA, into a 4-bedroom ranch-style brick home. I was in heaven—I finally had my own room! My brother had his own room, I had my own, and my two younger sisters shared a room, though my baby sister mostly slept with me. I was practically her second mother. I couldn't be Keo's second mother because she was only one year younger than me, and she actually wanted to be the big sister. She definitely acted like it too! *Smile*. I didn't care; I let her put on her pretend big-sister pants and do her thing. She was truly my first best friend and a fighter, too. We grew up around my family on my father's side, and they were all fighters. My sister and one of our cousins seemed to get into a fight almost every week. Me? I avoided fights at all costs. I mean, I could fight; I was just too scared. I thought my secrets might get found out if I fought. Anytime someone said something out of line or seemed to want to fight, my sister was right there, ready to stand up for me.

My favorite boy cousin was like that too. He didn't play around when it came to me; he protected me and didn't hesitate to "punch someone's lights out" if they crossed the line. Meanwhile, I did my best to make sure neither he nor my sister got into any trouble if I could help it. I hated fights. My big cousin is only about six months older than me, and we used to go over to his house all the time. They lived in a trailer in Rochelle, GA. Their house was always fun and never boring. My cousin didn't even know how much I needed his protection back then. Then again, he probably did—after all, I was so fragile and timid, so nice and sweet that anyone could run over me or pick on me without me defending myself. But my favorite cousin didn't let that happen. No one took advantage of me or picked on me when he was around. And if he wasn't around, he would definitely find out about it and straighten things out later.

I took pride in helping him with his homework, and he didn't mind defending me when it was necessary. Helping him with his homework was my way of showing appreciation, and I wanted nothing more than for him to succeed in life without getting into too much trouble. I was definitely different from all the other girls in the family. They all looked at me like I was bougie or something, but in reality, I was just frightened of life and people. So, I would rather they think I was bougie than know what I truly was.

My siblings and I would often spend the weekend with our cousin, whom we called "Auntie." She was actually an older cousin, but it was kind of a ritual to call her auntie. She had a deaf daughter about our age, so it felt strange to think of her as just a cousin. For a long time, I truly thought she was our aunt. It wasn't until I was a teenager that I learned she was really our cousin. I was a late bloomer in knowing family relationships because I didn't care to get to know new family members; I just wanted to be close to my momma. Everyone loved hanging out at Aunt-Cousin's house. She was cool and made everyone feel loved. Don't get me wrong, she had her rules and stuck by them. If we disobeyed her, she followed through on whatever punishment she set in place.

One particular day, my siblings and I stayed over at her house. She told us we had to be back inside before the streetlights came on, or we would no longer be allowed to spend the night. We could still visit but never spend the night again. On that day, my brother went off on his own. My baby sister stayed at the house with the adults because she was too young to roam the streets. My younger sister and I walked around town. We stopped by other family homes and waved at school-aged classmates but didn't really stop anywhere. We decided to stop by my uncle's trailer before we headed back to Aunt-Cousin's house. This was my father's brother, and they could almost pass for twins—that's how much they looked alike. He was probably everyone's favorite uncle, the one with jokes for days. I am speaking in the past tense because he passed away—I think it was cancer, which is very prevalent on my father's side.

We stopped by his trailer to say hello before heading back to Aunt-Cousin's house. Just as we were about to leave, Favorite Uncle called me to his back room, saying he wanted to give me something. Thinking nothing of it, I went back with him. He handed me a small teddy bear. I said, "Thank you." But I was shocked, immediately trembling and feeling uncomfortable. He asked, "Did you see what I just did?" I said, "Yes." He made sure I understood what he did. So, he brushed the back of his hand across my breast again. I was mortified. My beloved uncle touched me. Not once, but twice, and he wanted to make sure I understood what he was doing. I had hoped it was a mistake the first time, but when he did it again and asked if I knew what he was doing, there was no doubt in my mind. I backed off and hurried outside to my sister. We stood by his trash can, and I told her what happened. She burst out laughing and called me nasty. I hadn't even done anything. I didn't want the bear or to be touched. I even offered to give her the bear, but she pulled back and said, "Hell no, I don't want it." So, I threw it in his trash can.

All these weird, familiar feelings started popping up, so I asked my sister if she wanted to stop by a classmate's house on the way back to Aunt-Cousin's house. I needed the distraction; I couldn't go back to her house feeling so vulnerable. We ended up returning late and never spent the night there again. After that, she became just "Cousin" to me. She had lost the "Aunt" respect, and only "Cousin" respect remained. My sister and I tried to explain why we were late, but she didn't want to hear it. She packed our things, took us home that night, and told us she loved us. I was so hurt. But I thought maybe it was best that no one knew about what Favorite Uncle had done. I definitely didn't want anyone mad at me. I was only about 10 or 11 years old. What was I supposed to do? We were taught good touch and bad touch in school, but at home, we were taught to keep our mouths shut and not tell family business. I certainly wasn't going to snitch on Favorite Uncle. He was family.

I was never a fan of airing out my encounter with my favorite uncle. So, this is the first time I am airing it all out about my encounter with my uncle to my family. My sister was only a year younger than me and knew just about as much as I did…nothing. I did realize years later that his sisters, probably brothers, and maybe older nieces and nephews could have known. I overheard my eldest aunt tell one of the family members in a joking way, "You better not let your kids sit on his lap." I immediately started tensing up. That got me thinking: did they know he was touching little children and chose to "sweep it under the rug"? Did they know that he did it to me? Was he the only one in the family that was molesting family members? So many unanswered questions. I was *sooo* heartbroken. I mean, this was the error where you kept your mouth shut and didn't tell your family business. What goes on in your home stays in the home. I still loved my family, but I felt like I couldn't trust any of them. I definitely wasn't going to tell them what happened to me now because they already knew what he was capable of doing. Needless to say, my children were never brought around him. I never blamed the family for what he chose to do. I loved them even more but didn't trust anyone around my children. However, I did become close to his son. I mean, it wasn't his fault his father was interested in small children. I definitely didn't want him to hate me because of his father's actions. So I never told him; I just loved him even more.

I was really hurt about the outcome of my aunt-cousin. I looked up to her. Still do. I use some of her techniques for raising a family within my own family. My whole perspective on life just changed even more. I still carry around the values of love, life, and family that she taught me. I hate that I carried that hurt for so long because she never knew what happened to me while we were under her care. We even carried children together. I was pregnant with my firstborn while she was pregnant with her lastborns (twin girls). We even christened our daughters together on the same day, at the same time, in the same church that we grew up in. Although we didn't talk regularly, she showed me love every time we met, and I showed her love too. I will always love my aunt-cousin. I am grateful for the life lessons that she taught me. May her beautiful soul continue to rest in peace.

Chapter 6

Sweet Memories

My childhood wasn't always bad. I have some sweet memories of happy days that my brain didn't automatically bury, memories that I hold dear to my heart. It's funny how my brain works. I wasn't even aware for a long time that my brain was packing away my memories. My siblings and I would reminisce about the "good ole childhood days," and I had difficulties remembering. So, I would pretend to know what they were talking about. I was embarrassed. My brother used to pick on me all the time, even still to this day, saying I have a bad memory. I knew I didn't have a bad memory; I just couldn't figure out why I was having a hard time remembering certain events from my childhood. During counseling, I discovered that my brain was working for me. I had been living in flight mode my entire life, packing away events and leaving room only for bad memories so I could maneuver through life with extreme caution. I didn't do such a good job of that, but I somewhat succeeded.

I love music, but I hate rap. I get so angry when I hear rap. For a long time, I couldn't understand why. I don't know the song because I was so young, but my brain remembers it was rap. My mother's younger sister used to listen to her Walkman daily. She would grab her Walkman, go stand in the middle of her dirt driveway, and dance and mumble. I could tell it wasn't rap because she used to wind her hips, and I would be out there winding with her and trying to keep up with her mumbles. Every time we visited, I would anxiously wait for her to grab her Walkman. I knew what that meant. I think she knew too because I could see her watching me follow her, but she would pretend like I wasn't there. I don't know why, but that was amusing and fun to me. I felt like she enjoyed it too because it was basically our routine. We would visit, she would grab her Walkman, put on her headphones, and start mumbling and winding those hips, and I would be out there with her, winding and mumbling.

My siblings and I used to run in the fields. This was before our baby sister was born. My mother was pregnant around this time and would work in the fields while pregnant, which led to her going into labor two months early due to working so hard in the fields, resulting in my baby sister being premature. Back in those days, there were planes that flew over the fields, dropping chemicals on whatever plants were growing. We felt like we were being chased by the pilots because the fields were full of vegetables, cotton, or fruit. We would already be out playing in the fields when the planes would appear, seemingly trying to drop the chemicals over our heads. It was fun to run from the plane's path as it dropped those chemicals. We stayed in the fields, playing and working. It may be hard to believe, but my brother, younger sister, and I used to help my mother and grandmother earn money. We got a little money for helping out. It was fun to work in the fields and play in between, and even more fun to receive a few dollars in pay so we could go to the store later on and buy $0.01 candy. We would pick cotton, peas, okra, peanuts, and pecans. We weren't allowed to help "throw" watermelons in the watermelon fields because that was a job for men only. The closest we girls got to the watermelons was picking one out to eat over the weekend.

I recall staying with my grandmother in the country of Pulaski County. My grandfather was living with her at that time, though he was hardly ever home. We loved to raid his room to get some good ole $0.01 candy from the store. He knew we were taking his coins. He never said a word; he just kept on replacing what we took, which was his spare change. My grandfather couldn't read, but that man could definitely count money. We stayed in his room, counting the money we collected as well. We would run out as soon as he came home, though. He was not crazy. He was not allowed to walk through the front door, so his room was in the very back of the house connected to the kitchen, which were the only two areas he was allowed in. So, he mainly only came home to rest. Those were some scary days. My grandmother used to always warn us to stay out of his room. I don't remember who warned us, but we were told that he did not sleep in his bed but in a casket under the bed. I thought the family was just talking trash about my granddaddy. He was cool. He didn't say much and let us take all his loose change.

So, one day we were told not to go in the back room because Granddaddy was in his casket sleeping. It still feels like a dream. As children, when you tell us not to do something, we're going to do it to find out why or if there's any truth in the stories told, like my mother seeing the man on the moon, a headless horseman, and a witch riding her back for trying to save her sister from that witch. Those were the days. Anyway, a few of us went into the back room to see if Granddaddy was actually back there sleeping. Well, he was not in his bed. So, we did what any curious children would do. We looked under his bed. Boom. There he was, sleeping under the bed in a wooden box that looked just like a casket. My youngest aunt, brother, younger sister, and I screamed at the tops of our lungs and ran out of there like our lives depended on it. My grandmother laughed so hard when she saw us running for our lives and yelled, "I told y'all to stay out of that man's room!" That was one scary but fun moment. Needless to say, we have not seen his casket in that room under the bed anymore.

Chapter 7

The Separation

My mother was pregnant with me when she married my father. I was her second child and his first. At birth, I was diagnosed with a heart murmur and a trait of sickle cell, which has since been renamed hemoglobin C. I can only imagine how afraid my mother was to hear that news. My siblings all had a clean bill of health, so everyone had to watch out for me to make sure I didn't overexert myself. My baby sister was born prematurely but was still very healthy. That was a very happy day for me. It was also a scary day because my mom went into labor early due to working in the hot fields while pregnant. We'd get dropped off at my grandmother's house for the day, and I could hear my grandmother yell, "Don't be out there working too hard in that field while you're pregnant." She'd say, "Yes, ma'am, I won't." The next thing we knew, she was being rushed to the hospital because her water broke from picking up those heavy bags of vegetables. It was a scary moment but a happy one because we all finally got the chance to meet our baby sister, Suela. I was about to be a big sister again. This moment felt different because I was getting the chance to actually be a big sister. I mean, I was already a big sister, but my younger sister, Keo, was closer to my age and felt more like a best friend than a younger sibling. We did everything together. She was my ride-or-die. But with my baby sister, it was a different feeling. I could actually help Momma raise her. I was able to hold her, feed her, change her diapers, bathe her, clothe her, teach her, protect her, and more. When my mother brought Suela home, all she had to do was focus on healing and tending to the baby at night or while I was in school. Other than that, Momma didn't have to lift a finger.

Rob was the firstborn. I was the second. Keo was the third. And last, but not least, Suela was the baby girl. And man, was she one spoiled little girl. I did my best to keep her in line, but my parents didn't care to discipline her at all. I mean, we (the oldest three) got beatings every single day. It didn't matter who did what; when one person got in trouble, everyone got in trouble. My father didn't hesitate to get out his brown leather cow belt and beat us one by one because we should have been there to keep each other out of trouble. Most of the time, I stayed in the house, and he would yell my name, "It's your turn, Tia." I'd cry, saying, "But I wasn't even outside." He'd respond, "Well, you should've been out there with them to make sure they didn't get in trouble." And he'd beat us for what seemed like forever. It would take my mother saying to each child, "Alright, Walt, that's enough." She only whooped us when it was absolutely necessary. So, because we took all the beatings while our parents just laughed at the things Suela did, I'd occasionally pop her on the hand or her behind. Someone had to make sure she didn't turn out bad. She did whatever she wanted, and nothing happened to her. She was a charmer and highly cute but devilish in the same breath. She once had me running through the hall screaming and crying because she couldn't get her way, so she bit me on the butt and wouldn't let go. Instead of my parents helping to get her off, they burst out laughing. I was about to knock her on the head to make her let me go, and the first thing they yelled was, "You better not hurt my baby!" How unfair was that? Needless to say, I got her back later on for biting me. I couldn't sit down for a whole day. I can laugh about it now, but it wasn't funny then.

Suela knew she could get away with anything. She was such a little charmer. She had everyone wrapped around her tiny fingers—everyone except me, of course. I did spoil her to an extent, but I wasn't gonna let her get away with murder. My goal was to teach her right from wrong so she wouldn't get the wrong impression. I think I did pretty well. She still grew up an extremely spoiled girl with big confidence, but she knew the world didn't revolve around her and that her actions had consequences, good or bad. Because she wasn't disciplined by our parents like her older siblings were, she carried a different kind of strength. We were terrified of our father. Suela, on the other hand, was not. She had no problem talking back to him, swinging on him, or doing whatever she felt necessary at the time. My parents' abusive relationship didn't affect her the way it affected us, though it still affected her. She could defend our mother in public, whereas we only defended her through wishful hoping, huddles, and tears. There are so many memories of us cowering in a corner or our room until all the madness was over. Not Suela. She'd be right in the middle of it all, and I'd have to go in and grab her to make sure she didn't get "accidentally" hurt in the middle of all the chaos. We had so many sleepless nights, wet pillows, snotty noses, and unsettling dreams. It affected us all daily. We never knew when something would pop off; we just made sure to stay out of the way. Fear was definitely front and center for the oldest three. Suela didn't experience the same fear, which made her brave. I would've loved for her to beat him up, but I knew her strength was no match for his. I was actually happy she had the courage to jump on Daddy's back and threaten him for hitting our mother. I admired her bravery.

We were living in a four-bedroom, one-bathroom brick house in Pineview, GA. I don't recall why, but one night, we (the girls) decided to sleep on the pull-out couch in the living room. I think Rob was sleeping in his room. Anyway, we were awakened by screams and crying. It was clear our parents were at it again. Those screams and cries were all too familiar. We very slowly and carefully opened our eyes just enough to see our mother run past us and out of the house with no clothes on. She was naked, running the streets, knocking on neighbors' doors, begging for help, with Daddy on her heels. I don't recall if he was naked or not. I do recall her coming back inside because no one would help her. I guess they were just as used to her screams and cries as we were, so they weren't going to involve themselves in a revolving situation. Back then, I didn't understand why no one wanted to help Momma. I used to think they were probably scared of Daddy, too, like we were. Who knows the real reason? I never bothered to ask.

There was another incident in the same house where they fought in the living room. We were right there, huddled up together and crying as usual. Not Suela. She was the brave one. She did what I always did in my head but never in reality; she jumped on his back, started punching him, and screamed, "Get off my momma!" It was in that moment that I think my mother found a little more strength because Daddy knocked Suela off his back without realizing what he'd done. When he did realize it, he stopped hitting Momma and left for the night. I grabbed Suela to make sure she was okay. Momma was stunned, death in her eyes, but relieved her baby girl wasn't hurt. That may have been the beginning of Momma's strength and a big eye-opener to how her children were being affected by the chaos.

It was the summer of 1995. In the middle of the day, everyone was doing their own thing—chilling in a room, watching TV, playing game consoles, or whatever kids did inside back then. My parents were both in their room with the door shut. I figured they were doing grown folks' stuff. Suddenly, I heard my mother screaming for us to come open the door. My baby sister was ready to run and open it, but I held her back because I heard my father say we better not open that door. Instead of listening to our mother, fear overcame us, and we all huddled on the couch in the living room, crying and holding back our fearless baby sister. The very next day, our mother instructed us to pack our clothes for the rest of the summer. We got dropped off at my grandmother's house. She had moved out of the country and into the town of Hawkinsville, GA.

I was so worried about my mom. I'm sure my other three siblings were just as worried. She was in Pineview, GA, all alone with no one to protect her while we were bunched up in Grandma's house with her younger children and other cousins from time to time. We called our grandma "Ma," too. We still do to this day. Sometimes, I'd yell "Ma" when they were in the same room, and they'd both say, "Huh?" It was so hilarious. It still tickles me.

Well, that summer visit turned into a home for me and my siblings, starting at age 11 until I turned 22 and had my first child. That marked the end of watching my mother be beaten by her husband—my father—and the beginning of us scrambling for meals and clean clothes. My mother turned to the streets, coping with the pain and loss of a good nursing home job. My father was furious that she decided to leave, wanting to make her life a living hell, and he did just that, hurting us all in the process. We lived with her and were constantly around to witness the drama. He threatened to take us from her, showing up at her job and making a scene, which caused her to lose her job. That made it even harder for her to find new work in any nursing home with the cloud of drama that followed her. It was a bad breakup.

My mother told us it wasn't our fault that she and our father separated and that we should always love our father despite what they were going through. I respected her for that; she never put us in a position where we felt like we had to choose between our parents. I was grateful for that because I loved both my parents and definitely didn't want to choose. My father, on the other hand, was not as understanding. When my mom finally allowed us to visit him after things calmed down, he cursed her out to us every chance he got. I was too afraid to tell him I didn't appreciate it. It wasn't until he got locked up that I found the courage to speak my piece through a letter. He had a year behind bars, and during that time, we wrote to each other frequently. Even in his letters, he cursed my mom, calling her every name except a child of God. But because he was behind bars, I felt brave enough to write back and tell him how I felt about his disrespect.

On paper, I was able to be brave, telling him I didn't appreciate him calling the mother of his children names to his own children. I explained that we understood what was going on between them and that our mother had confirmed it wasn't our fault. Through it all, she never, not once, soiled his name to us. Even to this day, she doesn't speak badly of him and still caters to his needs. Whenever he needs someone to check up on him, she won't hesitate to make a trip to ensure he's okay. Just because we weren't living with him full-time didn't mean he couldn't take care of us. For some reason, he felt my mother took that opportunity away from him. I explained to him as a child that he could still meet our needs, whether we lived under the same roof or not. I admit it felt good to finally express how I felt. Since then, I've never had to hear him disrespect my mom in front of me again.

We were poor, but we had a decent life. Once my mother left my father, though, it felt like our lives spiraled downhill. We barely saw her. She was no longer raising us the way she had; she did her best to raise us partially while also chasing drugs. It was no secret—the whole town knew my mother was a drug addict and alcoholic. Everyone knew, except me. I don't know why

I was so blind to the signs that were there. I guess I didn't understand drugs, and I was a mama's girl. When I found out, I was torn, heartbroken, and in shock. In the blink of an eye, we went from being raised with love and care to depending on the streets to fill in the rest. We slept on floors in family members' homes and shared a can of baked beans with my younger sister just to keep food in our bellies. My brother was in and out of juvie, trying to escape the madness, and I thought my baby sister was trailing my mother. But then, in my 40s, I learned she was actually being dropped off at friends' homes while Mom did her own thing. So, really, Keo and I were left to fend for ourselves.

Each of us has our own story, but to me, baby sis and big bro ate well. Keo and I, not so much. I wasn't thinking about the struggles they could have been facing; all I could think about was how they were eating good meals while I had to share a can of beans to survive. Sometimes, we went to friends' or family's homes just to make sure we ate at least once a day. It was embarrassing, draining, and hard to deal with as a teenager. We also had to light candles at night because the lights were often cut off. We boiled water on plug-in stove tops to take hot baths because the gas would be turned off too. We carried jugs of water from the neighbors' houses to stay clean and to flush the toilet at least once a day because, at times, our water got turned off. We'd eat sugar bread as a snack because we couldn't afford real sweet treats. We made sure to spend time with family and friends during the day to eat a decent meal during summer or school breaks. We definitely had to be present at school for breakfast and lunch because we might not have food for dinner.

All this pressure was placed on my plate at 12, trying to make sure my baby sister felt as little of the blow as possible, not knowing she was going through her own trials when Mom took her out with her and left us at the house. Whenever we had her with us, we used her charm to help us get certain things we needed. That little girl could charm the fur off a bear during hibernation season. It was lovely, until she tried to turn that same charm on us. LOL. We made the best of the life we were given. It has molded and shaped us into the women and man that we are today.

I tell you, living in a two-parent household was stressful. It was hard watching my father come home bloody sometimes and drunk. Sometimes, he didn't even make it home after getting locked up for various reasons. Or witnessing our father walk in the door and get into a big physical fight with our mother. That was never easy to watch or hear. There was even a time when we witnessed our father having to drink out of a straw because he was jumped and stomped so badly that his jaw got broken. He had to write out what he wanted to say or use what little sign language he knew to communicate with us. I heard the stories behind it and made sure I stayed out of the way of racism or anything that could make people mad because I didn't want to get harmed myself—or worse, killed. I feared for my father's life a lot. I also feared for my mother's life. I loved them both and didn't want anything bad to happen to them. I would cry all night every time something happened. Watching both parents bleed from the top of their heads because they were both hit with a bat was traumatic. My mom went to the ER while my dad stayed home and dealt with the pain, and my sister, brother, and I huddled behind one of the cars in the backyard, crying. We didn't know what to do, and we were scared the guy would follow us back to the house and finish the job. Our little lives were filled with drama and trauma that we had no control over.

In spite of all this, it was also hard living in a single-parent household, which eventually turned into another two-parent household. We were struggling really bad. Sometimes, I wondered, was our life better in an abusive home, or was it better knowing we were poor, trying to survive mentally, spiritually, and emotionally while keeping it all together in an unstable living situation? What I am sure of is that my childhood life seems so surreal today. Were we really that poor? Did we really sleep wherever we could, at my aunt's and grandmother's house? Were we really struggling to maintain our sanity as children? Did we really move one to two times a year for nearly 15 years? Were my parents really drug addicts and alcoholics? Life was definitely hard, hitting us every which way, but somehow, we all managed to maneuver through the life that was given to us. We still have a ways to go, but we are putting in the work and making better decisions than what was taught to us. Some are more progressed than others, but I'll take some type of progress over no progress at all.

Chapter 8

Moving On

In 2002, I graduated from Hawkinsville High School. That was the first accomplishment that I was extremely proud of. I was the first in my family to graduate with my high school diploma. For me, this meant that my siblings had a chance to become better than our environment. It meant that we didn't have to follow in our parents' footsteps and drop out due to life circumstances. It meant that I could be a light and an inspiration to my two younger sisters and my older brother—that we were no longer a product of our environment. We were going to start living life and stop letting life live us.

I was living with my grandmother at the time that I graduated. I took the summer off to kind of ease my mind and build up the courage to go and live on campus for my first year of college. COLLEGE. I was always told that I would grow up to be someone great. I was the one who never had faith in myself that I would even live to see the day I could tell others I was going to college. It was others who saw my greatness because I, myself, felt unworthy and hopeless. I felt like I needed to win. I had to win. If I won, my family won. My mother won. My father won. My brother won. My younger sister won. My baby sister won. And my future family won. Everyone connected to me would win. This mindset gave me the strength and willpower to keep going. Whatever I had going on, I would not, could not, give up.

I am just so grateful and thankful for everyone who shed light on my situation and spoke life into me. I hold onto those encouraging moments and use them as part of the tools I need to stay motivated. My survival was bigger than me. Me surviving the life I was given and the pain that I had to endure temporarily by myself was bigger than me. My whole family was affected, and I felt like they needed me to be that guidance to show that it was possible to live a better life. I was going to be that example for them, no matter what.

I woke up every day in awe of even being able to still breathe. It's crazy because I got bullied from elementary school all the way up to the 9th grade. I was picked on because I was a nerd. I was told my breasts were too big to be in kindergarten and that I shouldn't have even had breasts. I was literally the only kid in kindergarten with boobs. That was *sooooo* embarrassing. I remember being in third grade, and it was the first time ever that I recall calling someone my best friend. Somewhere down the line, she felt the need to join the many others and try to bully me. We fought in the bathroom. I held my own. We never spoke again. I never fought anyone again either, until I got to the 9th grade. I hated getting in trouble. That fight we had in the bathroom was just she and me. I can't say I won nor lost. I will say we never rekindled our relationship after that. I also didn't get into any more school fights. I did fight cousins and siblings, but school fights were out of the question.

By mid-9th grade, I was fed up with life and people. I no longer feared fighting in school or after school. I became silently reckless. No one knew I was suicidal. I did crazy things to try to take my own life. I just wanted all the pain to go away. No one liked me. I sure didn't like me. It just seemed like everyone wanted to use me, abuse me, or make fun of me. So, I would jump in front of moving cars. Those people had some good reflexes because everyone would stop in enough time not to hit me. I took half a bottle of Tylenol. We didn't have anything stronger than that. I would drive around a long curve with a steep hill going 100 miles or more. It was fun—reckless, but fun. And I recall trying to slit my wrist with the sharpest knife in the house. It was a dull knife. We were so poor that we couldn't afford anything sharper than that. I was so disappointed. I can honestly say I didn't know anything about living or dying. Every suicidal attempt I made, I failed at it. My life was so bad that I couldn't even kill myself properly. So, I even gave up on that. All I knew at the time was that my life was worthless and I wouldn't be missed at all.

I felt ugly. I was told that often by my peers. So, I would wake up and try to find beauty in the mirror. I knew I had a good heart. I just couldn't find that physical appearance that was supposed to match up to my inner being. I was also told by a few people that I was a beautiful young woman. I admit, I saw that beautiful young woman maybe twice a week. I would even go as far as seeing "her" for an hour out of the day. My mentality was really screwed up. I still have moments, even to this day, when I look in the mirror and may see the beautiful Tia or the ugly Tia. I never know which one I will see. I pray each moment I see the beautiful one so that I can gaze in the mirror at my beauty instead of wondering why I am ugly today or at this moment. She only appears in the mirror. I can tell only in my reflection which one is present. I look back at my high school pictures and wonder why in the world I thought I was so ugly. I was actually BEAUTIFUL. I still am, for that matter. But I didn't understand nor did I know how beautiful I was until I turned 30. That was a monumental moment, and I haven't looked back since.

Chapter 9

Motivation

After my first year of college in 2003, I moved into my first home. It was a two-bedroom, one-bathroom tri-plex. It wasn't the best first home, but it was mine. I was dating a guy at the time. In all honesty, he was the reason I got the place. Otherwise, I would have moved back in with my grandmother. My sister had moved to Warner Robins after she graduated. My brother was still in and out of prison. My baby sister was still with my mother, who eventually ended up in foster care.

That was not such a good relationship, but I am grateful it happened because I got out on my own. I was so scared of life. Him lying to me, saying he was homeless, was just what I needed to get a place for us both to live in. We stayed there for about six months together and then broke up. I found out so much about that man from living together. He really was sweet but a big liar. I just couldn't deal with all that. I was told if you lie, you will steal. If you steal, you can kill. I didn't have time for any extra drama in my life. I turned my back on my family because of that relationship. When I realized what was happening around me, I had to get out—and fast. So that was the end of it. We parted ways, and I lived in that location by myself for a good while. I was never lonely because it was the hang-out spot. There was always someone there—either due to me doing hair or because someone wanted to hang out. It was great—until I fell into yet another traumatizing event.

I have had so many of these situations occur to me, and it's just so unbelievable. Anyway, I started dating my future husband while living in my first home. To me, it was fate. I was crushing on him in high school. To him, I was probably a life ticket. He says he was crushing on me too, but I find that hard to believe. No one really liked me. The boys were all interested in me because I had big boobs. Sexual assault for the majority of your life will definitely do that to you. I got pregnant in 2005 and had my first baby girl in 2006. This birth changed my whole perspective on life. I was living just to be living. Her birth actually gave me a purpose. I no longer had to live just to live. I now had a little one to look up to me and give me the love I had been yearning for. I was so quiet growing up that all the aunties, uncles, and cousins overlooked me. I was the good girl, so I didn't need much love. It was my Aunt P who saw that I needed nothing but love.

At the age of 22, with my first child, I was in a confusing situation. Right before I started dating my future first husband, I was hanging out with a few friends. There was one in particular that was really cool. I guess I gave off the wrong vibe by letting him come over whenever he wanted to and chill. He was, at the time, a really good friend. That was all I saw him as. He and others would come over to chill, drink, smoke, and rap like a normal day. I had a karaoke machine, and all the homies came over to spit rhymes. To me, it was a place of serenity for them, instead of hanging on the block, getting harassed by the police, or doing things to get them in trouble or jail time.

Anyway, I heard stories about how alcohol brings out the real person. Not only that, I have a past where my goodies were taken on numerous occasions, and nothing was done about it. So, one particular night, I got back home from one of my weekend excursions with a long-time friend. I would go when she needed a designee to be there so she could party with no worries. I would take a weekend sabbatical with her and visit her aunt and party for the weekend. Midtown was as far as I had gone. I had never been to Savannah. I may have been only 30 minutes away and just never went. I had the opportunity to go, but that probably would have ended badly for me, so I'm glad I didn't go. So the last time I decided to go away for the weekend, the homies stayed at the house. I didn't really have any valuables, so I didn't mind them staying there. I did leave my friend in charge because I wanted to come back to a house in order and not a whole mess.

I was already being accused of sleeping with him. I got accused of sleeping with a few of my homies, but little did those females know I wasn't interested in any dudes I grew up with. My interest was towards guys from outside the town I grew up in. I braided the guys' and girls' hair, conversed with them, or just hung out in the same areas. I was affiliated with these guys only on a friendly level, but others didn't see it that way. And that particular night, this one person everyone so loved didn't see it that way either. I had no interest in him. I was just being overly nice without thinking there would be any consequences. No one taught me how to be vigilant and cautious of the company I kept, so I was naïve as to what was about to go down.

I made it back home, and the few people who were left in the house were told to leave, but he stayed behind. He was pretty wasted, so I assumed he was going to sleep over. I think I told him he could have the room and I was going to sleep on the couch. Now, why would I do that? He was so aggressive and persistent with me that night. I was laughing nervously but so scared on the inside. The more I denied him, the more aggressive he got. After so many "no's," it was very apparent to me that he wasn't going to take no for an answer. I didn't know how aggressive he was going to get, so I became very afraid and nervous. So, to keep him from getting too upset and more aggressive, I gave in and let him have his way with me. I'll never forget what he told me after he was done. "You wanted it." I was so hurt because I thought we were really friends. I thought he respected me and our friendship. That night killed our friendship and left me so confused. I went years trying to process everything that happened that night. I was too afraid to tell anyone because he was loved by so many. He was at my house every single day. People already assumed we were together, so I would've seemed crazy saying he raped me. Who was going to believe that? I couldn't even believe it myself. But that was my reality. So, I distanced myself once again from everyone and tried to push the hurt and pain down. I still find myself processing the situation and wondering what would have happened if I had been a stronger person. It's unsettling how I tense up in uncomfortable situations and revert back to that 4-5-year-old little girl. I should have been taught to fight back. I should have been taught about the cruelty of the world. I should have been taught how those closest to you can sometimes be the main ones to hurt you.

I went on with my life and started dating shortly after that awful encounter. I informed my then-boyfriend that I was probably pregnant and didn't want him to be surprised or confused about who the father was. I told him the situation, and he assured me he had my back, that I wouldn't need to chase down the father because he would be there for me and my unborn child. I took the first pregnancy test, but I didn't know how to read it. I took it to my old friend (the assailant), and he read it, telling me it was negative. I felt it was too early to tell. About a week or two later, I took another test, and it came back positive. I just knew it was his and not my boyfriend's. So, for five years, I thought this guy fathered my oldest daughter.

It turned out he was right, and I was wrong. My heart dropped because I had no idea what was going on. It wasn't like I wanted him to be the father. I was upset because I had told her who her father was and took her to see his mother and father from time to time. I was embarrassed because I had gotten it wrong. So, I had my boyfriend tested, and he turned out to be the father. That was a relief. I knew I hadn't been with anyone else, but if my rapist wasn't the father, how could it be my boyfriend's when we were using condoms? So, I thought. I gathered myself and made necessary phone calls to everyone involved, apologizing for my mistake. No one was upset with me and respected my honesty. I never explained why I'd claimed the wrong father. I couldn't allow that to hold me back. I had a beautiful baby girl to look after and love unconditionally. She needed me just as much as I needed her. I felt like I had made a fool of myself, not knowing my boyfriend was the actual father. My young, inexperienced mind thought it had everything figured out but got it wrong.

So, I was left to pick up the pieces by myself because, by this time, my boyfriend was upset and done with the situation; he had initially asked me for a blood test. I didn't understand why he wanted one then, but I do now, though it's too late. Even with tests showing he is the biological father, he refuses to claim our first child. I was young, had just been raped by someone I thought was a friend, and thought using condoms would avoid confusion over who the father was. So, I was sure of it in my mind. After chasing down this man for a blood test for five years, I finally had results for both men. Luckily, my boyfriend was the father. By that time, we'd already had our second daughter. I swabbed the ex-friend, swabbed myself, and sent in hair from my boyfriend to get the results I needed. I had both girls tested by my boyfriend to settle any doubts. I was a mess but relieved. I didn't have to live with a horror story of how my child was conceived.

I put on my big-girl pants and called both men's mothers to give them the news. I hated myself for raising my daughter to believe the wrong man was her father while we'd been living with her true father. The other mother was sweet and understanding; she acknowledged that mistakes happen and asked if I would continue to bring her around. I couldn't do that. I had to let go for my daughter's sake and avoid further confusion. She still says, to this day, whenever I go back to my hometown, that she remembers the house she used to visit. But I felt it was best not to continue the relationship, knowing what I knew and feeling how I felt. I decided it was best not to keep her confused about how she had three grandmas. Besides, I needed some healing, and cutting all communication was the start of that journey to get my life back in order. I mean, who would have believed me if I had spoken up at the time? He was at my house every day, and everyone loved him.

Even the other women he forced himself on admitted to me that it had happened to them, too, but no one ever spoke up. Even though I have documentation, he still refuses to believe he is the father. I mean, it was his idea to get tested, so I did, and that was the result. It wasn't like I was freely giving my goodies away. I got caught in a bad situation, and he ended up my knight in shiny armor. I handled everything as a child would, and now here I am on marriage two. I ended up marrying the father of my girls after being together for four years. We had a baby boy as well. We spent 12 long years together and were married nine of those years. I even went as far as getting our son tested too because we never stopped arguing about him being the father of our first child. I don't understand why he kept arguing, but he did.

My children were my lifeline for a very long time. I didn't love myself, but I loved them with every breath in me. Right before I got pregnant with my son, I started seeking help. I was so tired of being angry all the time. Tired of harboring so much pain. Tired of feeling ugly, worthless, defeated, and good for absolutely nothing. I started going to these meetings with a group called Life Changers back in 2009. This group was connected to a church whose name escapes my memory. But oh, what a true blessing this group was. I don't even know if they realize how much of an impact they actually had on people's lives. When I tell you my life was definitely changing, it was. This was the first time I got a taste of relief. A little weight was lifted off my shoulder. This was the first time I felt safe enough to tell my story. Through the fear, I felt a little relief in sharing how I was rapped numerous times by multiple men, known and unknown, from the age of 4 or 5 to around 30. I felt like a bullseye target. It seemed like men knew that I was self-conscious and if they took what didn't belong to them, I wouldn't say a word. For the most part, they were right. I don't know what was going on through their heads; I just knew that they knew I was the perfect target. I even lost count of how many times this horror story has happened to me. I no longer can remember the faces. They appear sporadically, but if I sit and try to remember, I always forget some instances. It's to the point where I am forgetting the faces, names, and occurrences. I have trained myself to block the memories that I can't retrieve when I need them most.

I often ask myself, if I had told my mom and aunt exactly what my first boy cousin was doing to me, would I have been raped in my own home twice by two different people at different times whom I thought were my friends? Would I have been molested by my uncle? Would my mother's friend have been brave enough to molest me when she allowed him to stay with us when he had nowhere else to go? Would I have been raped at a house party with my sister and friend at that same party? Would I have been raped by a complete stranger in my car? Would I have been butt-raped twice by my husband at the time? Would I have stayed in a toxic relationship as long as I did? Would my brain be in a constant fight or flight mode?

So many questions. Lord, this is deep. Stop and breathe. I hate that my life was how it was, but then again, I wouldn't even be here writing this book and pouring into the lives of others. I am grateful that God decided to spare my life and show me grace and mercy on a daily. I did a lot of things I am not proud of, but one thing is for sure: I am supposed to be here. I figured that out the hard way. It took me attempting to take my life about four failed times. It wasn't until I had my first child that I began to look at life differently and actually wanted to live, not for me but for her and my possible future children.

Chapter 10

The Straw That Broke the Camel's Back

I can say that I had an okay marriage the first time around. Although I was young, I still understood order and submission. Compared to what I was used to seeing growing up, I thought my marriage was a success. I knew what I would and would not put up with. The deal breaker for me was cheating and anything that would be life-changing. I may be repeating myself, but I had a huge crush on my ex-husband in high school. I was so shy back then. We would walk right past each other in the hallway, and I would hold my head down so he wouldn't see me looking at him. I was in the 10th grade, and he was in the 11th. He only attended my school for one year, but it was enough time to grasp my attention from afar.

Fast forward, I moved into my first apartment in my second year of college. I was living in this tri-plex apartment for a year with an ex-boyfriend. That relationship was toxic too. He lied from the time I met him to now. Lying is just something he loves to do. I ended up getting the apartment under the manipulation that he had gotten kicked out by his parents and was homeless. So, I got us a place to live. The only thing I am grateful for out of that relationship is that I got out on my own and didn't move back in with my grandmother. Now, we did have some great moments, but the whole relationship was based on a bunch of lies, and I just couldn't see myself dealing with that for the rest of my life. I was already deeply damaged, but I still had morals and some respect for myself. I didn't think I deserved anything good in my life. I definitely didn't deserve the best, but through it all, I had to preserve something just in case something came my way. I had to find a way to be in control of my own life. Dealing with liars and cheaters was a hard no for me.

Roughly six months after we moved into the apartment, I ended up single and readily available to explore life. The lies had finally caught up with him, and I was not going to hold myself back or stay in an uncomfortable situation any longer. So, for one whole year, I was free to be me and choose life however I wanted to, with no one holding me back. Besides, as a teenager, I was diagnosed with a heart condition called Mitral Valve Prolapse. The doctor told me to stay clear of stressful relationships and avoid getting pregnant due to the strain it could have on my heart. I took those words to heart. Being that I was born with a hole in my heart that eventually closed up, contracted asthma as a teenager due to my parents smoking cigarettes around us all the time, and had a dysfunctional valve, I was scared. So, I really took heed to avoiding stressful relationships. I would date guys, and as soon as they caused too much friction, I was out of there. I was already dealing with unknown mental issues, newly developing health issues, and poverty. I was not about to deal with any guy who would make my chest hurt and my nerves rattle. That one whole year of fun quickly came to an end when I saw my high school crush's face after a two-year sabbatical. I was immediately taken away by his beauty and the memories of walking past him in the hallways with my head facing the ground but my eyes cutting up toward him so I could admire him without him ever knowing. Later down the line, he told me he was admiring me as well in high school. I don't know if it was the truth or a lie, but I do know it was very intriguing to hear.

So, because of who I was at that moment in 2005, I made it clear that I was interested in being in a relationship with him. I was just a little hesitant because I had just been raped a week or two before we had sexual intercourse. Being that a condom was not used, I was certain that my assailant was the father. So, I asked my boyfriend to use a condom for at least three months to be sure and make no mistakes about who had fathered my first child. I know that might have seemed fast, but I was so used to being victimized that I did not know how to stop and process what was happening. All I knew was that I had to keep going because if I stopped, that would be the end of the world I was living in. My life would have been over. So, there was no room to stop or bask in the hurt and pain that I was suppressing.

It is funny, though, because after my first daughter was born, my boyfriend at the time asked me if he could take a blood test. Of course, I said no because I was dead sure who had fathered my baby. Besides, we used a condom for three months, so how in the world could he have been the father? How could he think that there was even a possibility that he was the father? I pondered these questions, but I didn't sit on them too long because I had everything in place, crossed all my T's, and dotted my I's.

Well, five years later, after my chasing, begging, and pleading, my assailant finally agreed to a blood test, and lo and behold, he was not the father! This left me in tears, confusion, and disbelief. There was no way that the results came out as 99.9% not related. My method was flawless and foolproof. It turned out that I was the fool. At least, that is exactly how I felt. I immediately started making all the necessary phone calls and apologizing to those who were involved and deserving. Some I didn't care to call because there were so many negative people in the midst of what was going on without even truly knowing what was going on and why I was dead set on believing that he had fathered my first child. I truly believe I was his target because I had mentioned in a friendship conversation that whoever I had my first child by was going to be stuck with me forever. That is how I felt because I wanted children, but not multiple fathers. So, later that day, I sent out an additional sample to have my boyfriend tested just to see if he could have been a possibility. I was really racking my brain, like: did someone rape me recently, did I volunteer to have sex with someone before my assailant, and I didn't recall, or could my current boyfriend truly be the father? I was so out of it. I honestly didn't know what to think or how I should even think. My mother-in-law brought me back to reality, though, when she stated, "Shouldn't this be a good thing that he is not the father?" Ding. Lightbulb. I then realized that it was more out of being embarrassed because I had to have been living with the father the entire time. As soon as I sent the sample in, the results did, in fact, come back that my current boyfriend, who asked me for a blood test, was 99.9% the father. By this time, five years later, he had drilled in his mind that he was not the father and still believes to this day that he is not the biological father of my firstborn child. Either way, I was going to continue to be the best mother I could be to my daughter and give her all the love I never had.

I learned a lot from growing up in an abusive, dysfunctional, and broken home. In spite of everything I had experienced, I vowed that I would do all that I could to not let my children go through what I went through. I was determined to break chains and change the narrative of my future. I was not going to be a product of my environment or my past traumas. I refused to raise my child and future children as such, either. So, I knew I had to make some changes within myself. Little did I know, I was breaking some chains and unknowingly reliving others. I was an angry Black woman who refused to allow any man to control, manipulate, or abuse me. I was raised in an era where beating your wife was normal, and everybody minded their own business. When I became an adult, it was still very much apparent, but more women fought back, neighbors called the police, and/or wives left their abusive husbands. This was not going to be me. "I'll get him before he gets me" was my train of thought. It turned from me slapping my boyfriend to him nearly knocking me out. I even got a black eye once because I tried to hit him with a 2x4. I don't recall the reason why I grabbed the board, but to me, it was needed at the time. I held my ground. I never showed him any fear though. Mainly because I blamed myself for the fights. He would do things like leave the door unlocked with my nephew inside, and I would haul off and slap him for endangering my nephew. I've gone so far as putting a knife to his throat and hitting him with my car because our arguments got so out of hand and violent.

At one point, I wanted out. I knew that we were in a very unhealthy relationship, and I was putting my children in the same situation I was in growing up: watching my parents in an abusive relationship. I actually thought the violence was not so bad or effective at one point because we only fought some of the time, and I wasn't beaten to a pulp like my mother was. I actually blamed myself for the hits because, at one time, in the beginning of the relationship, I started the hits. Yes, I eventually realized that I was just finding excuses to stay because we had three children together, had gotten married, and I still very much loved him. He was my husband. Our vows said, "Through thick and thin, sickness and health, until death do us part." I was all for the "til death do us part" of it. I even went so far as to tell him those exact words. His eyes lit up, and he was smiling like he had struck gold. and stated, "Now that's how you know someone really loves you." I was confused. I was disturbed. I was coming to the realization that this was not love. Why should I have to threaten him to prove to him that I love him? This was definitely not the life that I wanted to have. I knew I was on the wrong path and had created a relationship that I vowed I would never end up in. Besides, we argued all the time in front of the children. Not only did it damage me, but it was damaging them as well. To be honest, although they were young, I believe they were relieved we split up because they saw the hurt and the pain I was enduring. They were enduring some of it too. I knew that much because I had been through it myself in my own childhood.

I mean, I had left the relationship on numerous occasions, but I always ended up giving in to him, begging me and the children to come back and that he promised to do better. He spent a lot of time drinking, smoking, partying, gaming, and God knows what else. I didn't have time to chase him, so I focused on loving me more and raising our babies. By loving me more, I could build up the strength to leave him and move on to a better life without him. Although we were married, and I was preparing to leave him, I still loved him; I just was no longer "in love" with him. I wanted nothing but for him to succeed in life. I did my best to build him up while it seemed like he did his best to tear me down. He acted like he was jealous of who I was becoming. I was a wife, full-time worker, mother, and full-time college student striving for a better life. I was not okay with where I was at in life, so I did everything I could possibly do within my reach to change the life I was living in order to have the life I wanted to live. I thought we had the same goals, but apparently we did not. He had the audacity to tell me I wasn't anything but a toilet scrubber with a master's degree. I was a housekeeper by day and went to college at night or on the weekends. I even had the pleasure of dropping the children off with their grandmother when her son was not around to help care for his own children. I can proudly say that she has her master's as well. She knows and understands the struggle with juggling school and life. All I have to say about all of that is, "LOOK AT ME NOW!"

I confided in one of my sisters in Christ, and she helped me realize that my very own husband was jealous of me and that I had outgrown him. His mother told me that in the beginning of our relationship, I was going to outgrow him. I thought she was just talking trash because their relationship was rocky. I thought she just didn't want him to be with a good woman and that I was going to give him all the love she had neglected to give him. Well, let's just say Momma knows best. We are now the best of friends (mother/daughter), and I can tell her with ease that she was right and I was wrong. But again, she understands life and how cruel it can be. Nevertheless, I got so tired of bringing myself back down to that poor, useless little girl who had no voice and was too ashamed to speak up. I wanted a better life for me and for my husband, but little did I know then that you can only help those who want to help themselves. I knew something needed to change, and it had to start within me. I was so much more than all the bad things he said I was and what I believed at the time. I thought I needed him to help me be stronger and more confident in who I was. I looked for him to help me come out of that dark place I was in, but he only seemed to push me further and further into it. I know I was looking in the wrong direction. I just had no earthly guidance.

So, at the age of 27, I started going to a group called Life Changes in Warner Robins, GA. This was the beginning of a healthier, more vibrant me. Besides, I was pregnant for the third time with my son and didn't need him to grow up thinking it was okay to beat on women and belittle them. I also needed to show my two girls that they were not born to be punching bags either. They needed to love themselves so they could choose the right person to love them back and be submissive as a wife and a wonderful mother if they decided to have children. I always told my son he was going to be a great husband and a wonderful father. Life Changes was the first realization that I was worth living a good, decent life. I needed to love myself first in order to properly love anyone else. This program taught me how to go about loving myself and that I needed to write this book to share with the world what I've been through and how I'm getting through it.

On my 30th birthday, after saying "I love me" in the mirror daily for a whole year, along with some other affirmations, I woke up fabulous. I looked in the mirror and chanted, "I love me. I am beautiful. I am smart. I am worth it." I said these words regularly for an entire year so that I could live it and believe it, especially on my birthday. It definitely worked and was the best birthday gift I could give to myself. At 30, I finally saw a very beautiful, smart, attractive young woman. From that day forward, my self-esteem has been rising, and my light has been shining. This drew an even bigger wedge between my husband and me. I've learned that in your growing season, everyone can't come with you. It is possible to outgrow people. Everyone cannot come with you on your new journey. Some will get left behind, some will come, and some will join the movement. It would be nice, but as it is written in the Bible (NIV, John 15:2), "He cuts off every branch in me that bears no fruit, while every branch that does bear fruit he prunes so that it will be even more fruitful." I constantly pray for God to remove those from my life who don't belong and to help me continue to become a better version of myself so that His light can shine through me. Therefore, I have lost a lot of people on this journey to self-love and happiness. And I am okay with that.

Sometimes, I feel like I didn't leave my husband at that time quickly enough, or else I wouldn't have had the awful pleasure of knowing him to become a child molester. There was no way I was going to stay with him after that horrible discovery. Before this, we didn't have a lot of bad days. As I said before, we fought on several occasions. I, for one, thought we were getting better, and I no longer needed to prep for separation because we had finally gotten to a good place. I had just started counseling with the YMCA. The arguing had subsided. We were both working and making plans to buy a house together. The children were doing well in school. We were sexually active on a regular basis. Then, BOOM, everything I knew was stripped away, and my children and I lost our loved one. I lost a husband, and they lost a father. Our world was turned upside down, but luckily, we had a massive support system that held us up and helped me so that I could help my babies get through our loss. I was like Job from the Bible. I had built an empire, and that was taken from me. I could not see a brighter future, but I also knew, in the very back of my mind, that I was not going to stop or I would die. I couldn't stop; I still had three little ones who depended on me. I needed to get them through the loss first. I had to protect them and their emotions. I had to help them learn how to navigate through life. I had to show them that they did not have to live in trauma, loss, fear, helplessness, defeat, embarrassment, sorrow, or any other feelings that would show up during hard days.

I will say that my brother, younger sister, and a newfound friend played a major role in making sure that we at least survived that first year. That was a huge loss for us—the only father our children knew and the only man I knew for 12 good years of my young adult life. That was a big change but well overdue and highly necessary. I had been on a healing journey, trying out different programs and counselors since the age of 27. I mastered puppetry. My mind was the controller, and my body was the puppet. Now that a lot of things have come to light, I am still in the process of learning my body. I have learned that life is not all traumatic. It is not just filled with hurt and pain. Life can be filled with so much love and joy, sunshine and rain. I know I've had some good days—lots of good days. But my heart was filled with so much disappointment and no direction that I could barely enjoy the good old days. I am still learning so much about loving me. Although I hate the trials and tribulations, I am blessed they have helped me to be able to help others in their times of need. I am learning to live life and see the outward beauty in me. I know I am beautiful inside. I know that one day, when I look in the mirror, I will no longer see the ugliness but full-throttle beauty. This story is definitely a continuation.

I am now married for a second time with two additional babies and still working on loving me. Life is not all peaches and cream, but it is the life God chose for me, and I am to do my best to make the big man upstairs proud of His child. This life is mine to live, and I plan on doing just that—LIVING IT!

A Letter to My First Assailant

Dear Cousin,

Although you were not the beginning of my trauma, you were definitely the beginning of my life, going in a downward spiral effect. You were very aware of what you were doing to me. Shame on you! How could you take my innocence? What made you think it was okay to try to ruin my life for your pleasure? Granted, you almost did because I felt unloved, useless, suicidal, confused, helpless, and dirty. But God! I can't recall a lot that transpired, but the little that I do know plays a major part in my life choices and feelings. I hate that my aunt died so tragically. But I am glad she did not witness the son she birthed. Why did you choose me? Even to this day, you still reach out to me. WHY? I do not want anything to do with you. You are banned from my life, my children's lives, and their children's lives. You are dead to me. I am gaining the power back that you stole from me. You deserve everything you get and have coming your way. Yes, I am still very angry. I thought I forgave you, but I honestly have not. I don't know how. I have tried over and over again to have forgiveness in my heart for my own healing, but it just ain't happening. I fear there were some others before me and definitely after me. May God see fit your punishment for harming little girls and possibly little boys and women. Maybe in the future, I'll ask God to have grace and show mercy, but as of today, July 7, 2022, I am not there. I'd like for you to burn eternally in hell, but that doesn't seem befitting. So, as usual, I'll let God handle you. Just stay away! Let me be just as dead to you as you are to me.

YOU WILL NOT WIN

I wrote this letter in 2022, and the words still sting and still feel so alive. I don't have as much hate in my heart, but I do very much want nothing to do with him ever in life. Forgiveness is not coming as fast as I would like, so I am just continuing to take my healing one day at a time and learning how to live with the trauma in a better, healthier aspect.

A Letter to My Ex-Husband

Dear ex-husband,

My life has not been the same. I keep asking myself, "What could I have done differently? What signs did I miss? Why didn't I trust my gut? Did I have any part in the decisions you chose to make? Why didn't I see the signs? Why didn't my children come to me?"

I can basically go on and on, but in reality, you made your decision because you wanted to. A father is a daughter's first true love. It was your job to protect your children, not harm them in any way, shape, form, or fashion. I thank God that he grabbed my attention when he did. There is no telling how long God has been coming to me, trying to warn me or just plain out grasp my attention. I hate you decided to permanently break up our family. But only God knew that you were not right for us. I mean, I knew it, but I was determined to make a failed marriage work. You had served your purpose in our lives. I am forever grateful for the three beautiful babies you have created with me. I hate I was left behind to pick up the pieces, but that's the hand I was dealt with. So, I'm going to continue to strap up my boots and put one foot in from of the other. My trust was betrayed. My love was revoked. My hard work in that marriage was spit on. Yet, I still didn't let it break me. I wondered why. Why didn't I fold like so many people told me that I should have? I imagine it's because my life was full of turmoil before you walked into my life. I was already a pro at internalizing my emotions. It was like one more destructive situation to add to my list. Your decision this time around was a different kind of low. It left us angry, upset, hurt, confused, distraught, and embarrassed. It was unfair. But here we are—healing, living, surviving, and working on forgiveness.

YOU DID NOT WIN!

I was so broken, lost, and, as usual, confused about how I should continue with life. I was not suicidal. My first attempt as a teenager was an epic failure. Although I am more educated and more successful in this day and age, if I were to try it, I love myself and would not do anything to harm myself or anyone else. I was left in a bad place and used my children to keep my head afloat. I needed them just as much as they needed me.

A Letter to God

Dear God,

Where do I start? I haven't the faintest idea, so I guess I'll start talking. I am supposed to be writing out a detailed letter on my shortcomings, wants, and needs. It's very difficult because as I am writing, I'm slowly losing memory of what I should be asking. I do know that my marriage is in trouble. The enemy has planted some deeply rooted seeds and I need them uprooted immediately. I know before, I asked to be shown how to fight for my marriage. But not like this. I know there has got to be a better way. I am a difficult person who wears her heart on her sleeves. I shut down easily. I don't like talking about my feelings or expressing them either. I can be such a knucklehead. I just hate opening up and then having my genuine concerns thrown back up in my face. I am still dealing with PTSD- childhood rape, molestation, bullying, and poor living in my younger years. On top of that, I have postpartum depression. I need a job with more money to better support my family. I need an attitude adjustment to be less quick to get angry or defensive. I want to be able to communicate my feelings and emotions effectively to be heard and understood. I want to love myself with ease and not a lick of doubt. I want to be able to give out that same love but in a healthier way. I love it way too hard and can't keep hurting myself. I want my husband to be less defensive (me too). Truly fight for a better version of himself and the life he wants instead of just talking about it. Be more confident in himself (I need that as well). Accept the love given and acknowledge the support given also. Support me in my illness. Be there for me like I am there for him. Listen to me. Hear me. Understand me. I need him to give out the same energy that he expects me to give out. We need to pray more as a family. Be more active. Be more empathetic of each other's issues. I want him to stop being so quick to run when issues arise. We need to come to an agreement when it comes down to parenting so that we can stand as one. I could try to be more happy and excited on my part with his accomplishments.

Lord, we need you in the midst of all these situations. It's been a while since I admitted that my faith has been shaken. Better yet, still shaken. It's been seven years, and I am still having major issues. God, I just want to thank you for putting each and every counselor I have had and or have in my path. Lord, I am asking that you continue to help me to be in a better place physically, mentally, emotionally, and spiritually. Lord, just be in the midst of it all. I know my brother has good intentions, but my ego and madness have interfered. Help me with that, Lord. This life of mine is super hard. I need relief. I need peace. I need unconditional love. I need compassion. I asked you for all of this, and you took away my first husband because he was not capable of giving me what I needed. So you gave me my second husband, Jason, to fill my void. Lord, if I wasn't or am not ready for him, let me know. I do think he is the blessing that I have been praying for. God, just intervene. I do want my husband. I do want my marriage. Just like Job lost everything and gained it all back tenfold, Lord, I am trusting you will give my family everything back that we lost times ten. I thank you, God, in advance for what you are about to do.

A Letter to My Husband

Dear Husband,

Thank you so much for coming into my and our children's lives. Thank you for adding three additional members—our oldest in California and the two little ones we made together. Our family is not perfect, but it is beautiful in so many ways. I love the accomplishments and growth that we have done and the obstacles that we have overcome. The enemy's job is to kill, steal, and destroy. We are both God's children, and I am grateful to have a God-fearing man like yourself to ward off the evil spirits of the enemy and do God's work. You came into my life as a divorcee with three children. You had one of your own. Our joining forces definitely made the enemy mad to the point where he pulled out the big guns. We are better and stronger than ever. Continue pouring into our children. Continue loving me unconditionally. Continue growing as a better person. You are beautifully and wonderfully made. I can't thank

God enough for placing you in our life. Life has not been the same since you entered it. It has no doubt had its ups and downs, but it has been a little more pleasant to maneuver through it with you by my side. I pray God continues to use you and anoint you. Keep doing God's work and be obedient to his calling. Life will lighten up for you and this family will hold up to the legacy you are creating and will leave behind.

I LOVE YOU

Being married is hard work, but it is pleasing in God's sight. I love my marriage. I love being his wife. God knew exactly what He was doing in preparing us for each other. We came into each other's lives broken but are healing. We are on this journey together, and there ain't nobody but God keeping us together, building and shaping and molding us as we serve His name on this side of heaven.

www.ingramcontent.com/pod-product-compliance
Lightning Source LLC
Chambersburg PA
CBHW050225100526
44585CB00017BA/2009